MATH FUN

TEST YOUR LUCK

by Rose Wyler and Mary Elting
Pictures by Patrick Girouard

JULIAN Ⓜ MESSNER

Acknowledgments

For good advice and practical help the authors thank
Dr. Robert Moll, Associate Professor of Computer Science,
University of Massachusetts, Amherst, Massachusetts.

Published by Julian Messner,
a division of Simon & Schuster,
Simon & Schuster Building, Rockefeller Center,
1230 Avenue of the Americas,
New York, New York 10020.

JULIAN MESSNER and colophon are trademarks
of Simon & Schuster

10 9 8 7 6 5 4 3 2 1 (hardcover)

10 9 8 7 6 5 4 3 2 1 (paperback)

Library of Congress Cataloging-in-Publication Data

Wyler, Rose.
  Test your luck / by Rose Wyler and Mary Elting.
      p.   cm. — (Math fun)
  Includes index.
  Summary: Presents mathematical recreations exploring the concept
of probability.
      1. Probabilities—Juvenile literature.   [1. Probabilities.
  2. Mathematical recreations.]   I. Elting, Mary.
  II. Title. III. Series.
  QA273.16.W95 1992
  519.2—dc20
    ISBN 0-671-74311-2 (library) ISBN 0-671-74312-0 (paper)
                                                    91-3919
                                                      CIP
                                                       AC

Hi!

One way or another, you keep trying your luck. Luck comes up in games, choosing sides, taking a chance, getting a job. The list could go on and on. Of course, you always hope for good luck, yet you know you can't count on it. For every winner, there is a loser, or many losers.

What can you expect? To find out, try these tests, games and teasers. They are so interesting you'll try them again and again.

If any grownups say you are wasting your time, tell them that you are doing math problems. Explain that you are studying the laws of chance just as Galileo and Einstein did. Then invite them to join you and test their luck too.

Win or lose, you'll have fun . . . Math Fun. We bet on it!!

Rose Wyler and Mary Elting

TABLE OF CONTENTS

The Power of Numbers; Lucky-Number Tests; Pick Any Number; The Thirteen Myth; "I've Got Your Number"; Magic Square Magic; Birthday Magic Square; Lottery Luck.

Which Hand?; The Nose Knows; Toss Up; Seven or Eleven; Fair Chances; Clever Princess; Why Dice Have Six Sides; Forgetful Coins; Penny Posers; The Pirate's Puzzle; Bingo Binge; Baby Bingo.

ARE THERE ANY LUCKY NUMBERS?
3794206184 85 ?

No one believes in magic any more. Yet many people think certain numbers work like magic. They choose these numbers expecting them to bring good luck in games, lotteries, and bets. But what are the chances that a chosen number will win? Let's find out.

THE POWER OF NUMBERS

The idea that some numbers are lucky is so old, no one knows when, where, or how it began. Maybe it was started by cave dwellers who had learned to count and had found that using numbers gave them great power. Then as time went on, different people began to believe that certain numbers were more powerful than others and might even bring good luck.

Some people thought that 3 was a lucky number, for important things often came in threes: father, mother, child; earth, water, sky. Others preferred 7. Japanese people believed there were Seven Gods of Good Luck, who were supposed to sail treasure ships into port on

New Year's Eve. The ancient Romans thought that 10 was lucky, because the gods had given people ten fingers to count with.

Even today, many believe certain numbers have special powers and can bring good luck. But is there any reason to prefer one number to another? What are the chances that a chosen number will win? As you will see, that all depends . . .

LUCKY-NUMBER TESTS

First, try a pencil roll and test six numbers. Use a six-sided pencil, and put a number between 1 and 6 on each side. Bet on one of the numbers. Then see if it wins and comes out on top when you roll the pencil. Roll the pencil 12 times and keep a score showing how many times your number wins. Get your friends in on this, and ask them to test different numbers. Does any number win more often than any other?

Since a pencil has six equal sides, each number has an equal chance to come out on top—that is, one out of six. With 6 rolls, you can expect your number to win once; with 12 rolls, you can expect it to win twice. Keep on rolling it, and that's about how many wins you'll get—one out of six. The same goes for the numbers picked by your friends.

Try dice, too. Each die has six sides, so when you roll one, you can expect a chosen number to win about one out of six times.

If you try a spinner with a disk divided into six equal parts, each with a number, the chances of winning are the same—one out of six. But what if the disk is divided into four parts? Or eight parts? Experiment with different disks, and invite your friends to test their luck with you.

How to make a spinner: take the top of a round carton and cut a paper circle the same size. Fold the paper into four equal parts. Number each part, 1 through 4, mark the center, then paste it on the carton top. Now take a pencil with a sharp point. Stick it carefully through the circle's exact center, and there's your spinner. When you use it, the winning number is the one touching the table at the end of a spin.

To test eight numbers, divide the paper circle into eight equal parts, then paste it over the first one.

PICK ANY NUMBER

Today many people still have a favorite number even though they know there really are no "lucky numbers." They pick that number whenever there is a choice, as this great mind-reading trick shows.

Start by bragging to your friends that you can sometimes read people's thoughts. Ask one of them—let's say, Suzy—"How about it? Can I try to read your mind?"

Suzy giggles. "You can try," she says.

Tell Suzy to think of a number less than 50 with two odd digits that are not the same. While you write 37 on a card, you add, "I can tell you're skipping numbers like 11 because both digits in them are the same. Right? Well, name your number. Now see if it's the same one that I've written down."

Suzy shrieks, "It is!"

Try the trick on other people. You will find that most of them pick 37. After all, how many numbers under 50 are made of two odd digits? Only eight: 13, 15, 17, 19, 31, 35, 37, 39. That gives you one chance out of eight of being right at the start of the trick. But when you mention 11, you steer people away from all numbers that begin or end with 1. That leaves three numbers to choose from, giving you one out of three chances to be right. Yet you're nearly always right.

Why? Maybe most people pick 37 because it ends with a 7, and 7 happens to be their favorite number. Is it your favorite, too?

THE THIRTEEN MYTH

How many people do you know who think the number 13 is unlucky? Ask your classmates, and see if any of them believe in the myth of "unlucky 13." Ask grownups, too. Many will tell you of a terrible thing that happened on the thirteenth day of the month, forgetting that unfortunate things happen on other days, too.

There was a time when businesses would not rent an office on the thirteenth floor of a building, and families did not like to live in apartments on the thirteenth floor. So the owners of the buildings simply numbered the higher floors 10, 11, 12, 14, and so on. Of course, nothing happened to the people on floor number 14, which was really number 13. Today the thirteenth floor is usually numbered correctly.

It's hard to explain why or how the number 13 got a bad reputation, for in some places it was considered lucky. In China and Egypt, people once thought it brought good fortune. In Belgium, women wore good-luck charms formed in the shape of a 13.

In the United States, the number 13 has a special history, for this country was formed by 13 colonies that banded together. This is why the American flag has 13 stripes. It is also why that number is used in different ways on dollar bills. On back of each one is a picture of a pyramid with 13 steps. Opposite it is an eagle holding 13 arrows and an olive branch with 13 leaves and 13 berries, and the shield in front of the eagle has 13 stripes.

If there *was* anything to the 13 myth, think how unlucky it would be to have 13 dollar bills—or 13 of anything, for that matter!

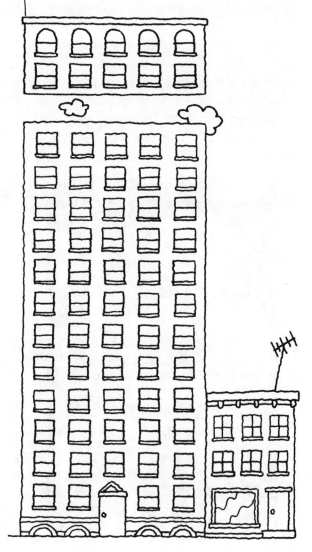

"I'VE GOT YOUR NUMBER"

"Don't try to kid me. I'm wise to you." Usually, that's what people mean when they say, "I've got your number." But those words once had quite a different meaning.

Long ago, people believed a special number went with a person's name. This idea probably started in ancient times when the Hebrews and Greeks used the letters of the alphabet for numerals. Since *A* stood for "1," *B* for "2," and so on, writing someone's name was like writing a series of numbers. Adding them up gave a special number that was the key to a

I'M JOE BOMBALLODADODADAY

THAT NAME MUST HAVE A LUCKY NUMBER!

person's future. The bigger that number, the more luck he or she would have.

Greeks who believed this claimed that luckily the hero Achilles had a name with a bigger numerical value than that of his enemy, the Trojan hero Hector. Achilles was destined to be the greater man, and that's why he won his fight with Hector.

It seemed that having a good name was helpful, but it did not always mean success. An enemy could misspell your name to give it a lower value, and that was supposed to put a curse on you. Or jealous people might boost the value of their names by adding letters or changing the spelling to make them luckier than you.

All of this was extremely confusing—particularly if you couldn't read or handle numbers. And in those days most people couldn't even write their own names. When in trouble, they sometimes went to fortune-tellers called numerologists, who made predictions by studying people's special numbers.

In making predictions, numerologists did several things with the numbers in a person's name. First, they added them. If the sum was a one-digit number, that number was used as the key to the person's future. If the sum had two or three digits, these digits were added. If the new total was 9 or lower, it became the key. If the total was over 9, the digits were added again to get a one-digit key number that could be used in making predictions.

This is what the key numbers were supposed to mean:

1—intelligence and reasoning ability

2—a sweet, sensitive nature

3—an original person

4—justice and balance

5—marriage

6—perfection

7—good luck

8—love and friendship

9—wealth and plenty

To see how this kind of fortune-telling worked, take these two names, Ada Beam and Solomon Levy, whose special numbers are 27 and 167. Since Ada's number is the smaller, she might have a less promising future than Solomon. But see what happens when the totals are reduced to single digits. Ada's number 27, becomes 2 + 7 or 9. Solomon's number, 167, becomes 1 + 6 + 7 or 14, which boils down to 5. So wealth is forecast for Ada and marriage for Solomon.

Just for fun, try this kind of fortune-telling on your friends. And if anyone thinks there's something to it, let them work out the fortune for Adolf Hitler. According to numerology, he turns out to be a nice guy!

A	B	C	D
1	2	3	4
E	F	G	H
5	6	7	8
I	J	K	L
9	10	11	12
M	N	O	P
13	14	15	16
Q	R	S	T
17	18	19	20
U	V	W	X
21	22	23	24
Y	Z		
25	26		

A	1	S	19
d	4	o	15
a	1	l	12
B	2	o	15
e	5	m	13
a	1	o	15
m	13	n	14
	27	L	12
		e	5
		v	22
		y	25
			157

MAGIC SQUARE MAGIC

If one number could bring luck, maybe certain combinations of numbers could bring extra good luck. That seems to be why magic squares became so popular.

According to an old legend, more than 4,000 years ago the Emperor Yu of China was sailing on the Yellow River. Suddenly he saw something strange—a turtle with Chinese numbers painted on its shell. There were nine numbers, arranged three in a row. What did they mean? Were they an omen? The emperor added them across, up and down, and diagonally. Each time, the sum was 15. Surely, there was some magic power in these numbers. Thinking they would

bring him luck, he ordered a charm made with the nine numbers on it, set in a square. He believed the charm really worked, and so he wore it all the time. And that's how magic squares began—or so the story goes.

At least one part of the story is true, for magic squares did start in China. From there, they spread all over the world. In India, they were hidden at the bottoms of bowls that were used in fortune-telling. Muslim doctors drew them on the feet of patients to ward off plague. Eastern Jews made them into religious symbols, since letters of their alphabet were used for numbers, and writing the sum 15 was the same as spelling the name of the lord Jehovah. Today, in Africa, women wear the squares on silk scarves. They also are painted on the decks of some cruise ships so that tourists can play shuffleboard. As it happens, shuffleboard numbers are the same ones that the Chinese used in the first magic squares.

4	9	2
3	5	7
8	1	6

ORIGINAL MAGIC SQUARE

Of course, not everyone believed the squares were magical. People who liked to play around with numbers found out

why the totals for the rows were the same. Then they began making squares based on other number combinations. Maybe you would like to try this, too.

First, take a good look at the square with rows that add up to 15. There are eight—three across, three down, two that slant. In four of them, the middle number is 5, and so the other two numbers in those rows add up to 10. That's all there is to it.

Well, now try making a square with rows that add to 18. It's easy. Just add one to each of the numbers in the 15-sum square.

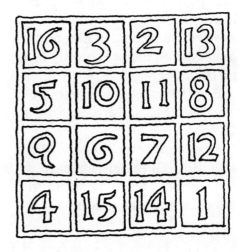

18-SUM SQUARE

5	10	3
4	6	8
9	2	7

What if each number in the 15-sum square is doubled so that the center square becomes 10? Will the square still be magic? And what if each number is multiplied by 3?

Can you make a square of nine boxes with rows that add up to 16? How about 27? Before you try, notice that the total for a row in a nine-box square is always divisible by 3, and the number in the center box is one-third of that total. If you try a total that gives a fraction when divided by 3, don't give up. Just be sure to use fractions in all nine boxes.

Making magic squares with more than nine boxes is possible, but tricky. A square of sixteen boxes was worked out by the great German artist, Albrecht Dürer, and then used in one of his pictures. In it, the rows add up to 34, and the four middle boxes add up to 34. The numbers in the two center boxes at the bottom give the picture's date: 1514.

BIRTHDAY MAGIC SQUARE

There is no limit to the number of magic squares that can be made. In fact, everyone can have a personal magic square based on his or her birth date.

Here's how to make one. Let's say it's for Eva, born February 5, 1980.

First, write the date the short way (2/5/80) under a square with nine empty boxes. Then fill in the boxes, using this guide:

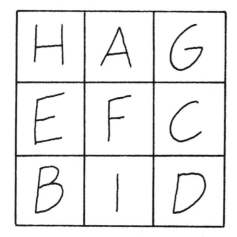

1. In the box that corresponds to A, write the year, 80.

2. Add the day to the year (5 + 80) and put the sum, 85, in box B.

3. Add the day to that sum (5 + 85) and put the new sum, 90, in box C.

4. Add the month to the year (2 + 80) and put the sum, 82, in box D.

5. Add the month to that sum (82 + 2) and put the new sum, 84, in box E.

6. Add the month to the number in box B (85 + 2) and enter the new sum, 87, in box F.

7. Add the month to that sum (87 + 2) and enter the new sum, 89, in box G.

8. Add the month to the number in box C (90 + 2) and place the sum, 92, in box H.

9. Add the month to that sum (92 + 2) and place the sum, 94, in box I. Now the square is complete.

Check Eva's square and you will find each row adds up to the same sum (261), which, when divided by 3, gives the number in the center square. In spite of the hanky-panky used in working out the numbers, you finally get a real magic square.

Try using your own birth date for a magic square. Make some for your friends' birth dates, too. Or show them how they can make their own.

Try the birth date of the United States—July 4, 1776—and you'll find that you can make a magic square from that or any other date.

91	76	94
90	87	84
80	98	83

Don't be surprised if you get hooked on magic squares. Lots of people have been fascinated by them and have invented special squares for special occasions. You will be joining their ranks. Happy Magic Squaring!

Here's a square invented by Benjamin Franklin that's full of tricks. Each row adds up to 260 while each half row adds up to 130. Tracing a slanting line up through four boxes and down four boxes makes 260. The four corners plus the four middle numbers make 260, and the sum of the numbers in four boxes making a square is 130. Clever Ben Franklin!

52	61	4	13	20	29	36	45
14	3	62	51	46	35	30	19
53	60	5	12	21	28	37	44
11	6	59	54	43	38	27	22
55	58	7	10	23	26	39	42
9	8	57	56	41	40	25	24
50	63	2	15	18	31	34	47
16	1	64	49	48	33	32	17

LOTTERY LUCK

YOU CAN WIN $10,000,000! . . . according to the ballyhoo that you sometimes hear on TV. Of course, you have to do certain things to enter the lottery and get a number. And usually, you have to be over 18. Well, suppose you do qualify. Then it's true you can win. But very likely, you won't. If 500,000 people are in the lottery, each with a different number, you have one chance out of 500,000 to win—and 499,999 chances to lose.

There may be a second prize. And in that case you have 499,998 chances of losing. Even if there are a hundred prizes, your chance of winning any one of them would be around one out of 499,900.

Are the lottery tickets given away free? Not exactly. When the lottery is run by a business, usually you have to buy something or have to subscribe to a magazine to get a number. If you really wanted the item, and were going to buy it anyway, the lottery ticket is gravy. You know you probably won't win, but it's fun to hope.

Lotteries, it seems, are good for business. Supermarkets sometimes give away lottery coupons with each purchase to bring people into their stores. Announcing a drawing at a given time and place can also be useful. Years ago, when the first long-distance buses appeared in Peru, Indians from the mountains were not used to schedules and often missed the bus. To get them to the station on time, one company added lottery coupons to the tickets and held drawings 15 minutes before the buses were due to leave. Soon both people and buses were leaving on time.

PARADA DE COMION

Raffles are a form of lottery. Most of them are held for good causes, such as hospitals, nonprofit radio and TV stations, food relief . . . maybe even for new uniforms for a school team. Usually the number of people in a raffle is much smaller than in a commercial lottery, so the chances of winning are greater. The prizes, although smaller, help sell tickets because people like taking chances.

Governments found that out ages ago. In the days of ancient Rome, the Emperor Caesar Augustus held a lottery to raise funds to repair the city. The Dutch rulers of the city of New Amsterdam, now known as New York City, held a lottery in 1655, but they gave out Bibles instead of money as prizes. The government of England ran lotteries, too. Perhaps the most successful one of long ago was the lottery that was held by the colonists to raise funds for the American Revolution. George Washington bought the first ticket, giving the lottery a great start. The amount collected was a lot of money for those days: $5,000,000.

More than 50 countries now conduct lotteries and more than half of the states in the United States run them to raise money for government services. In Illinois, ticket holders pick six numbers and have one chance out of 13,000,000 to win. New York State runs several lottery games with somewhat different rules and usually with big jackpots. A few years ago, four out of five of New York City's adults bought tickets for a lottery with a $45,000,000 jackpot!

State lotteries have become a business in themselves . . . in fact, a $15,000,000,000 business. Unfortunately, much of the money taken in—about 40¢ out of every $1.00—goes to the people who run the lotteries. They are the real winners.

In many states lotteries are run to help pay for the public schools. In case you live in one of those states, check on how much lottery money is actually used for education. Find out if the lottery has helped your school in any way.

FIGURING OUT THE CHANCES

If you play any game that depends on luck often enough, you'll win some and you'll lose some. Carrying a charm, like a rabbit's foot, won't help. Nor will rubbing the dice. But in some games a player has more chances to win than to lose. Let's look into this.

WHICH HAND?

Lizzie holds out two fists. A piece of candy is hidden in one of them. "Guess which one," she says. "And you get the candy."

The candy is just as likely to be in one hand as in the other. So there's one chance out of two to be right—or wrong. And if Lizzie was an octopus hiding a fish under one arm, there would be one chance out of eight to guess right.

Simple? Yes, as far as the math goes. But that may not be far enough.

THE NOSE KNOWS

Try some "nose reading" to tell which hand the candy is in. Ask whoever is holding it to stretch both arms out toward you, and watch the holder's nose. Usually, it will move slightly in the direction of the hand holding the candy.

The clue you get changes the situation, so that picking the correct hand is no longer a matter of chance.

TOSS UP

Toss a coin and one chance out of two it will land heads; one out of two it will land tails. Although you can't expect to land heads once in every two tosses, if you keep on tossing a coin the results will even out eventually. About half the flips will land heads, and about half will land tails.

Such results have led to the law of averages. To test this law, flip a coin 20 times and keep score of the number of heads and tails you get. You probably won't get 10 of each—that is, 50 percent heads and 50 percent tails. But get 20 kids (perhaps from your class) to each flip a coin 20 times. Keep score and see how many heads and tails you get in 400 flips. You still may not get 50 percent of each, but how close to that do you get?

You might also compare the percentages of heads and tails for the first 200 flips with the percentages for the second 200. Are they the same? How do they compare with the results for 400 flips?

Now suppose you flip a coin twice. What are the chances that you will get at least one head?

This problem may seem simple, but many great mathematicians and scientists were once stumped by it.

The problem first came up about 300 years ago, when gambling was a popular pastime among the aristocrats of Europe. In betting on how a coin would land, most people figured there were three possibilities if the coin were tossed twice. The two tosses could result in two heads, a head and a tail, or two tails. So there would be two chances out of three to get two heads. But heads turned up more often than that. Why, they wondered.

The scientist Galileo became interested. So did other great thinkers of the day. In tackling this type of problem, they showed that there are really four ways a coin can land when tossed twice. There can be two heads, a head and a tail, a tail and a head, or two tails. So there are three chances out of four to get at least one head—or one tail.

See for yourself. Try flipping a coin twice, repeating this 20 times, and record your results. Get some friends to join you and have a flipping party. You'll have fun checking on Galileo.

SEVEN OR ELEVEN

In a game with one six-sided die, there's one chance out of six to get any one of the numbers on it. But if a pair of dice is rolled, the player can get anything from a 2 (sometimes called snake eyes) to a 12 (a boxcar). Snake eyes can be made only from 1 and 1, and boxcar can be made from only 6 and 6, while most of the numbers in between can be made from either two or three combinations. Now, can you explain why the chance that a roll of two dice will show 7 is better than the chance they will show 11?

Here's how to figure it
out: These three combinations add up to 7: 1 and 6; 2 and 5; 3 and 4. But, you can also get 7 this way: 6 and 1; 5 and 2; 4 and 3, making six ways in all. As for throwing an 11, you can get that from 6 and 5 and 5 and 6.

So, the chance of getting a 7 is three times as good as the chance of getting an 11. To check that out, roll a pair of dice 30 or more times and keep track of the results.

FAIR CHANCES

"A buck to try your luck," yells Bill Bluster at the County Fair. "Roll three dice and you get a prize for any number of points under ten. The smaller the number, the bigger the prize! Try your luck, folks. Only a buck."

What's the catch, Roger wondered. He was sure Bluster was making money out of the game. That meant it was set up

so the players were more likely to lose than win. It also meant that the number of prizes given out was smaller than the number of dollars collected. As to the prizes, most of them were worth less than a dollar. Only those for 3 and 4 points were worth more.

Roger watched people play. Sure enough, there were more losers than winners. And none of the winners rolled 3 or 4 points. Why? What gave Bill Bluster such a big advantage?

As Roger watched people roll the three dice, he realized that the number of points that could be made ran from 3 through 18. Only seven of those points—3, 4, 5, 6, 7, 8, and 9—were under 10. Yet eight numbers—11, 12, 13, 14, 15, 16, 17, 18—were more than 10. That gave Bluster an advantage to start with.

Besides, all points over 5 could be made in several ways. Five could be made from a 3, 1, and 1, or a 2, 2, and 1; six could be made from a 3, 2, 1, or a 2, 2, 2, or a 4, 1, 1 combination. The higher the number of points, the greater the number of possible combinations. So the chances of throwing less than 10 were much smaller than throwing more than 10. Even smaller were the chances of getting 3 or 4 points. The only way to throw 3 points was to get 1 point on each die. To throw 4 points required a 1, 1, and 2, which showed up rarely. All in all, a great game . . . for Bluster.

CLEVER PRINCESS

Here's another teaser tale. It's about a strange law in the kingdom of Babur the Bad. Babur had ruled that a prisoner who was sentenced to death could toss a coin to decide how he was to die. "If heads come up, the prisoner will be shot naked," Babur declared. "If tails come up, he will hang in his clothes."

The first to be punished under the law was Princess Cleo. She had refused to marry Babur. In a rage, he ordered her death the next day.

"I have a big coin you can toss," he snarled. "Heads I win, tails you lose."

"That's not fair!" said Cleo. "I want a chance to win. What if I refuse to toss the coin?"

Babur laughed. "I will grant you a chance. To avoid being hanged or shot, you must appear in court neither naked nor clothed."

And that's how Cleo appeared. Guess how she did it.

Answer: In jail that night Cleo tore up her dress. Then she tied the shreds together and made a big net from them.

In the morning Cleo appeared in court wearing a big cloak. Babur asked if she was ready to toss the coin. "No," she shouted. "But I win!" Then she dropped her cloak. Wrapped in the net she had made, Cleo stood before Babur neither naked nor clothed.

WHY DICE HAVE SIX SIDES

L ong before there were coins to flip, people were trying their luck with dice or something like them. Almost 5,000 years ago, in a Near East kingdom called Ur, little pyramids, each with a different number of corners that were colored, were rolled in games. Later, in Egypt, people rolled small monkey figures. In Africa, they tossed decorated nuts or cowry shells and scored points according to the way the game pieces landed.

Now cube-shaped dice with dots for numbers have taken the place of the older pieces. Each cube is made with all six sides exactly the same size and shape, so that no one side turns up more often than the others.

Would it be fair to play a game with dice that have more than six sides? Yes, it would, if all the sides were exactly the same.

Twelve-sided dice would work; so would twenty-sided dice. But the six-sided cube is easier to hold and cheaper to make.

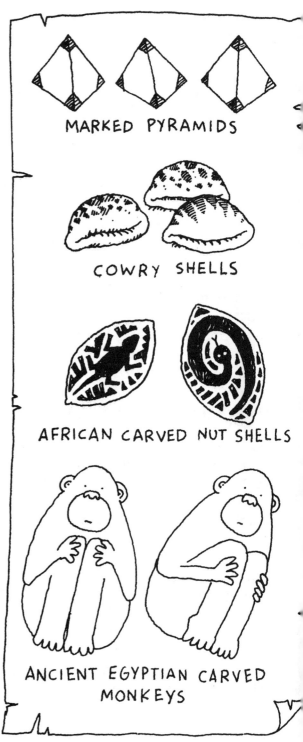

MARKED PYRAMIDS

COWRY SHELLS

AFRICAN CARVED NUT SHELLS

ANCIENT EGYPTIAN CARVED MONKEYS

FORGETFUL COINS

Suppose you toss a coin five times and it lands tails up each time. On the sixth toss, is a head or a tail more probable?

You might think a head would show up, and maybe one would, but one toss of a penny has no effect on the next toss. A famous French mathematician, L. F. Bertrand, explained this by saying a coin has no memory. If a coin cannot remember how it landed on one toss, how will it know which side to land on for the next one?

Coin flipping dates back almost two thousand years to the time of the Roman ruler Julius Caesar, who decided to have a picture of his head engraved on one side of each coin. Sometimes, when an argument started, a coin was tossed. If Caesar's head turned up, whoever had chosen heads was declared the winner, for the ruler could never be wrong.

PENNY POSERS

Ready to try some quickies now? The answers are on the next page, but don't peek.

1. How can you toss a coin so neither its head nor its tail shows up?

2. Sally and Jim were flipping pennies to see who could turn up the most heads. They played three games and each won two. How was that possible?

3. It's easy to get three heads or three tails to show using three pennies. But how can you get two heads and two tails to show?

4. This one is a groaner. It's all wet, but try it anyway. When does one toss of a penny affect the next toss?

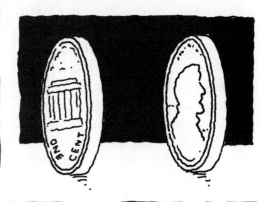

Answers:

1. Do a magic trick and vanish the coin. Then neither its head nor its tail will show up.

Try this one while sitting around a table with your friends. Just be sure you are wearing long sleeves.

Rest your left elbow on the table and lean your head sideways on the palm of your left hand. Toss a penny with your right hand and slap that hand over it. Ask, "Is it heads or tails or neither?"

"It can't be neither," say your friends. And for that round, they are right.

You try again. This time you pick up the coin by the edge with your right hand and turn to your friends saying, "Well, let's see what we have." At the same time, you edge your right hand toward your left sleeve and drop the coin into it. Now quickly slap your right palm on the table, pretending the coin is still there.

Look straight at your friends and say, "I don't think it's heads. Nor do I think it's tails."

Slowly turn your palm over and you are right—it's neither one. The coin has vanished!

2. Sally and Jim were not playing against each other. Each was playing against someone else.

3. Stand one penny between two pennies lying flat. The head of the standing penny should face the head of one coin and its tail should face the tail of the other coin.

4. When the coin is tossed into a river and lost, there is no next toss. Now don't groan. Didn't we say this one is all wet?

THE PIRATE'S PUZZLE

In the old days, pirates didn't flip coins. They grabbed them—as many as they could and whenever they could.

That's what Dead Eye Dick had set out to do when he boarded the Spanish ship *Isabella.* Dead Eye had heard there were three treasure chests in the hold. One was said to be filled with 100 bags of gold coins, one with 100 bags of silver coins, and one with 50 bags of each. Stealthily the pirate made his way into the hold. Sure enough, there stood the three chests.

"Yo-ho-ho!" said Dead Eye, reaching for the nearest chest. What was in it, he wondered. Gold? Silver? Both?

Dead Eye never found out, for he was captured and killed by the crew of the *Isabella.* But shed no tears for him—he's just a character in a teaser tale.

Here's the teaser: What were the chances of grabbing a bag of gold coins from the chest?

Answer: First, figure out the chance of grabbing a bag of gold from each one of the chests. Then add the results.

With three chests to choose from, there's one chance out of three—$\frac{1}{3}$ of a chance, you might say—to grab a bag from the chest with only gold in it. There's no chance to grab a bag of gold coins from the chest with only silver. And from the chest where half the bags contain silver and half contain gold, there's half of one chance out of three—that is, $\frac{1}{6}$ of a chance—to grab a bag of gold coins.

Add these chances (using $\frac{2}{6}$ instead of $\frac{1}{3}$), and you get:

$$\frac{2}{6} + \frac{1}{6} + 0 = \frac{3}{6}, \text{ or } \frac{1}{2}$$

So Dead Eye would have had $\frac{1}{2}$ chance—that is, one chance out of two—to grab a bag of gold coins. Yo-ho-ho!

BINGO BINGE

Bingo requires no skill, but once you start playing, it's hard to stop—especially if you munch on peanuts or popcorn as you play.

In case you have forgotten the game, this is how it goes: A caller is chosen at the beginning and given a bag holding 75 pieces, each marked with a different number. Every player gets one or more cards divided into five rows of squares. The center square on each card is marked FREE. The other 24 squares have different numbers on them, but no two cards are alike. Every player also gets a set of disks to cover numbers on the cards.

The caller's job is to shake the bag, pull out a piece and announce the number on it. Players with that number on a card, cover it or cover the FREE square. The first player to cover a row horizontally, vertically, or diagonally wins and shouts "bingo!"

At the end of each game, players may choose new cards and the winner of the previous game becomes the caller.

Although bingo is easy to play, you rarely win a game before more than twenty numbers have been called. Do you know why?

Here's why: Let's say you hope to win by covering the five spaces in the top row of your card. When the caller draws the first of the 75 numbers from the bag, there is one chance in 75 that it matches one of your numbers. When the second piece is drawn, there is one chance in 74 for a match, and so on.

To find the chance of getting five matches in just five drawings, you multiply: $\frac{1}{75} \times \frac{1}{74} \times \frac{1}{73} \times \frac{1}{72} \times \frac{1}{71}$. The result comes to less than $\frac{1}{2,000,000,000}$, showing you have less than one chance out in two billion to get five in a row.

How about filling up a row with FREE in the middle? Since any number that's called can cover FREE, you need only four different numbers to fill a row. Your chance to get all four of them, in four drawings is: $\frac{1}{75} \times \frac{1}{74} \times \frac{1}{73} \times \frac{1}{72}$. That comes to one chance out of about 30 million—still a very slim chance.

But there are many ways to win. When playing, you watch every vertical, horizontal, and diagonal row—27 rows in all. So by the time 20 numbers are drawn, you or some other player is likely to have a full row.

See for yourself and keep a tally for each game. That will show how many numbers are drawn before anyone wins.

Or would you prefer just playing the game? Bingo!

BABY BINGO

This game is also called baby-sitters' delight, because it keeps little kids busy for quite a while. If two people play it, use two cards, each divided into eight squares. Number the squares on one card from 1 through 8; on the other, from 9 through 16. Give each player eight disks to be used when numbers on his or her card are drawn from a bag, as in regular bingo. A third person calls the numbers, or players take turns in drawing them. This goes on until someone has a line of covered numbers and calls "bingo!"

For an easier game, use cards with only four numbers and a bag with eight pieces. For a harder game use cards with twelve numbers and twenty-four pieces. Or make up your own version of bingo.

THE MATHEMATICS OF MAYBE

Is the chance to win big? Or is it small? There's no need to guess. Laws of chance have been worked out and if you know how to use this kind of math, you can tell what to expect. As you will see, it's possible to measure the *size* of a chance.

THE NOBLEMAN'S PROBLEM

L ike other gamblers of his day, de Méré, a seventeenth century French nobleman, relied on his hunches. Maybe he would win; maybe he would lose. In fact, he did both. He made a fortune on his bets that a six would show up at least once in four rolls of a die. Then he lost his money betting on how often a double six would show up when he rolled two dice.

Upset by his losses, de Méré turned to his friend, the great mathematician Pascal, and asked him why some bets were better than others. Fascinated, Pascal took up the problem. Step by step, he worked out ways of telling what to expect when taking chances. In doing this,

Pascal started an entirely new kind of math—the study of *probability.*

See for yourself how de Méré's bet with one die works out. Pick a number—6, if you wish—then roll a die four times. If your number shows up at least once, score 1 on a tally. If it doesn't show, put down 0. Repeat this six times. See how often you score. Ask some friends to do this, too, and compare the results.

How did you come out? Since a die has six sides, when you throw it once, there's one chance out of six a chosen number will show. Yet there are five chances out of six it will *not* show. Throw the die four times and the chances of *not* getting it are:

$$\frac{5}{6} \times \frac{5}{6} \times \frac{5}{6} \times \frac{5}{6} = \frac{625}{1296},$$

which is less than ½. That means there's a better chance to win than to lose.

As you see, de Méré's bet was a good one, although figuring out the chances was complicated. But the "mathematics of maybe" is not always difficult. Let's see how it works in some simpler cases.

SILLY BILLY

Billy wasn't dumb. He just did silly things. On his way to school one day, he was stopped by the man who lived next door. "Billy, that's a strange pair of socks you have on," he said. "One is blue and one is yellow."

"I don't know why you think

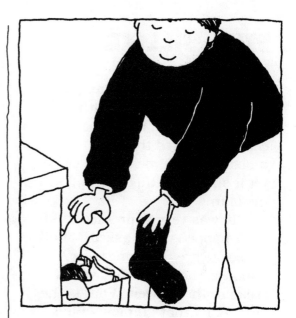

they are strange," said Billy. "I have three other pairs like them at home."

When Billy was getting dressed, there were four blue and four yellow socks mixed up with lots of other things in his bureau drawer. Billy had grabbed the first two socks he found.

What if Billy had grabbed three socks instead of two? Would he have had a matching pair?

Answer: Yes. Even if Billy didn't look at his socks, he would get a matching pair by pulling three out of the drawer.

Let's take this one sock at a time. Suppose the first one that Billy grabbed was blue. If the second one was also blue, he had a matching pair. If it was yellow, that wouldn't matter. The third sock would match it or match one of the others he had chosen, for there were only two colors in the drawer.

STILL SILLIER

The man who lived next door went over all that with Billy, but instead of calling it *chance*, he used the word *probability*. "It means the same, yet it's more mathematical," said the man.

Billy was very impressed. "But what happens," he asked, "if all my socks are the same color? Suppose I have just four yellow socks in the drawer. What is the probability that I'll pick a blue pair?"

Silly though it sounds, there is a sensible answer to that question. Try to figure it out.

Answer: With only yellow socks to choose from, there is no chance of picking a blue pair. So the probability is zero.

In math, when telling how much chance there is for an event to happen, numbers are used instead of words like *small* and *big*. Numbers are more precise. If an event cannot possibly take place, the probability is exactly equal to zero. If the event is a sure thing, then the probability equals one. And if the event is neither absolutely certain, nor absolutely impossible, the probability is between zero and one. It is a fraction, such as ½ or ⅓.

"Now do you understand?" asked the man next door.

Billy nodded.

"It's all quite simple," the man said. "When the socks in the drawer are two different colors and you grab two of them, the probability of a match is less than one. But if you grab three, the probability changes."

The next day, Billy tried the sock problem on his teenage sister. "Don't bother me," she said. "I wear panty hose."

"That means you don't know the answer," said Billy.

"So give *me* a chance to answer it," said his little brother.

And Billy did. But first he mixed up his blue and yellow socks and put four of each color in a bag. "Now guess how many you have to pull out to get a matching pair," Billy said. "Then start grabbing socks until you get two of the same color."

After trying this several times, Billy's brother was convinced that if you pulled out three socks, two would match. "This is a great game," he said. "Let's try it with five pairs of socks."

Since they didn't have enough socks, they put five strips of red paper and five of white in the bag. Now how many had to be drawn to get two the same color?

What's your guess? Draw strips of colored paper from a bag to check your answer. Then try the problem on your friends. It's a real puzzler.

Answer: The answer is still 3.

CHOCOLATE OR VANILLA?

"Take one," said Ann's grandmother, holding out the cookie jar.

There are 30 cookies in the jar: 10 chocolate, 20 vanilla. Ann wants chocolate. She hates vanilla cookies.

What is the probability that she picks the kind she wants?

Answer: With 30 cookies in the jar, Ann has one chance out of 30 of getting a particular cookie. Since 10 are chocolate, she has 10 chances out of 30, or one out of three, to get chocolate. So the probability that Ann gets what she wants is $\frac{1}{3}$—if she doesn't peek!

LUCKY STREAK

Sometimes it happens—you get five heads out of five tosses of a coin. But what is the probability of this?

Here's how to find out: First, consider the probability of getting a head on one toss. Since a coin has two sides, it is $\frac{1}{2}$, or one chance out of two. It is the same for the second toss—and for the third, fourth, and fifth tosses. The tosses have no effect on each other. They are separate events. So their separate probabilities are multiplied together to find the probability of five heads in a row. Work this out and you get:
$\frac{1}{2} \times \frac{1}{2} \times \frac{1}{2} \times \frac{1}{2} \times \frac{1}{2} = \frac{1}{32}$

If you use decimals instead of fractions and do the problem on a calculator, you get:
$.5 \times .5 \times .5 \times .5 \times .5 = .03125$.
That's the same as $\frac{1}{32}$.

You can work out the probability for any lucky streak of this type in the same way. See what a small chance you have of ever getting ten heads in a row—or ten tails, for that matter.

No records of lucky streaks in tossing coins exist, but there are records for roulette, a game played by choosing one of 38 numbers on a turning wheel. In a Puerto Rico casino some years ago, a man bet on the same number six times in a row and won each time. The probability of that happening is $\frac{1}{38}$ multiplied by itself 6 times—one chance in about 3,000,000,000!

CHARLIE CHAPLIN'S STORY

Charlie Chaplin, the funny little tramp in the movies of long ago, took his hunches seriously. At times, he suspected he had some kind of strange power that enabled him to make predictions.

He tells of one of these times in his book, *My Autobiography*. Chaplin was in a European bar with some friends when he noticed: "Three gambling wheels were on the barroom wall, each with numbers from one to ten. Dramatically I announced, half in fun, that I felt possessed with psychic power, that I would spin the three wheels, and that the first wheel would stop at nine, the second at four and the third at seven. And, lo, the first wheel stopped at nine, the second at four and the third at seven—a million-to-one chance."

The prediction was right, but Charlie's math was wrong. Was the probability bigger or smaller than he thought? Try to figure out what it actually was.

Here's how to figure it out: For each wheel with 10 numbers, the probability of guessing the right number is 1/10. Each guess has no connection with the next one. So for three wheels, each with 10

numbers, the probability is:
$1/10 \times 1/10 \times 1/10$.
This is equal to $1/1,000$. In other words, there is one chance out of a thousand. That's a lesser chance than one out of a million—a thousand times less, and so a thousand times more likely to be right!

What if only one wheel with 10 numbers is spun three times and a number is picked each time? The probability of guessing three numbers right would still be the same. But it would be different if the wheel had more numbers—or fewer numbers.

Why not try some number-guessing using your own spinner? (Directions for making one are on page 7.) Use a circle with 8 numbers and spin it three times, picking a number for each spin. Just remember that the chance of getting three numbers right is very small.

If you use a circle with 4 numbers instead of 8, you will have a much better chance of making three correct guesses.

Get your friends to join in and sooner or later someone will guess the right numbers on all three spins. When the guess is wrong, blame probability; when it's right, say it's luck.

Another pointer: In case grownups complain that you are wasting your time playing with a spinner, don't argue. Invite them to join you and test their luck. It will help, too, if you share the popcorn with them.

TESTING FOR ESP

Does the ability to read another person's mind exist? For many years, people have been doing experiments hoping to prove the answer is yes. They believe there is a way of getting information without using the senses of sight, hearing, smell, taste, or touch. They call this *extrasensory perception*, or ESP for short.

Ever since scientists began to study ESP, their progress has been hindered by hoaxes. Fakers put on demonstrations of ESP that seemed foolproof, yet they turned out to be just clever magic tricks.

Interest in the field faded until Professor Joseph Rhine started testing people with cards. He used a pack of 25 cards marked with five symbols: five cards had a cross, five showed a star, five had a circle, five had wavy lines, and five showed a plus sign. Anyone who tried to name the cards as they were dealt from the pack had one out of five chances of being right, and probably would guess five out of 25 correctly. So Rhine reasoned anyone who averaged better than that on several trials had some ESP.

After thousands of tests, records showed that a few people scored better than average. Did this prove they had ESP? Many scientists doubted that it did.

What do you think? Before answering, make 25 ESP cards, using 3 × 5-inch filing cards. Test classmates and neighbors, keeping track of the results. Can you find anyone who seems to have ESP?

Other scientists began giving ESP tests. Some of them got results like Rhine's. But suspicions were aroused when quite a few people made good scores. A careful check showed some of them were fakers who had found out which cards were dealt. Even worse than that, one of Rhine's staff was caught fixing up figures in an experiment.

So far, no one has been able to set up a foolproof experiment for ESP.

FINGER HUMDINGER

A simple ESP test can be made from an old kid's game called Finger, Finger. In it two kids stand back to back in front of a group of people. One player holds up from one to five fingers and the other guesses how many are shown. If a guess is wrong, the player is out; if it's right, he or she becomes the "finger man" for another kid.

To make an ESP test out of the game, you be the "finger man." Let each one taking the test guess how many fingers are shown five times in a row, while

you record all the correct guesses made. Repeat this for five rounds. In each round, since the test-taker makes five guesses, there's one chance out of 5 that one will be right. For five rounds, there are five out of 25 chances that 5 will be right (as in a deal with 25 ESP cards). A score over 5 supposedly shows ESP.

To show off your own ESP, ask somebody to give you the test. But beforehand, work out five secret signals with a friend who will let you know how many fingers are shown at least twice during each round. Then you will have the highest score—unless someone else is a better faker.

McMONSTER'S DINER

One evening, Mrs. Glob and her son Booby were headed to McMonster's Diner for dinner. The place was the hangout for all those who hated pizza, ice cream, and hot dogs. No junk food was served there: only wonderful yucky meals just right for hungry monsters.

For dinner, there were three courses: a salad, a main dish, and a dessert, and three choices for each course. Although there were nine things on the menu, a lot of combinations were possible. And, as an added attraction, McMonster's offered a free meal to anyone who chose the Lucky Yuck—the secret special combination of the day.

Here was the menu for that night:

Salads choice of posion ivy leaves, cactus greens, or thorny stems

Main Dishes Choice of roasted rats, creamed fish eyes, or bat burgers

Desserts Choice of spider pudding, buggy cake, or snail-slime pie

"I feel lucky tonight," said Mrs. Glob, as she placed her order for poison ivy, rats, and slime pie. "Booby, how about you?"

"Just three desserts for me. I think the Lucky Yuck is a fake.

There aren't many combos to choose from and nobody ever wins.''

McMonster overheard him. "You're wrong," he said. "There are more than twenty-five combinations, and I pick the winning one before we open. So everything is monstrously fair.''

Well, Mrs. Glob didn't win. But with three courses, each with three dishes, how much of a chance did she have to pick the winner?

Here's how to find out: How many different combinations of 3 things can be made from the 9 items on the menu? Take it one salad at a time. One salad can go with 3 different main dishes, and each main dish can go with 3 different desserts. As the diagram opposite shows, the salad can be used in 9 different combinations.

The diagram for each of the other two salads would look the same, for each one can also be used in 9 different combinations. So, with 3 salads, the total number of combinations is:
$3 \times 9 = 27$.

With 27 possible combinations to choose from, Mrs. Glob had

one chance out of 27 to pick the Lucky Yuck. Others eating at the diner had the same chance, too, for the winning choice was not announced until McMonster stopped serving dinner. As McMonster said, everything was fair, although it was true that with a probability of 1/27, few customers ever won a free meal.

By the way, the diagram used in working out possible combinations is called a *tree diagram.* The method, though simple, has a fancy name—*combinatorial analysis.*

Try it for 4 sets of 4 things—say 4 pairs of jeans, 4 belts, 4 T-shirts, and 4 caps —and count how many combinations are possible when you have 16 items. Do you get 136?

And how about 5 sets of things? If you don't want to bother making a tree diagram, get out your calculator and use arithmetic to work out the answer. After all, 5 things, each combining with 5 things gives 25 things, each combining with 5 things . . . well, take it on from there and you will get 3,125.

WOW!

Counting without counting—sounds impossible, doesn't it? But that's what combinatorial analysis is sometimes called. And with good reason, since a kind of math shorthand can be used in working out how many ways things can be combined.

Suppose you are lining up four kids named Tom, Ed, Sue, and

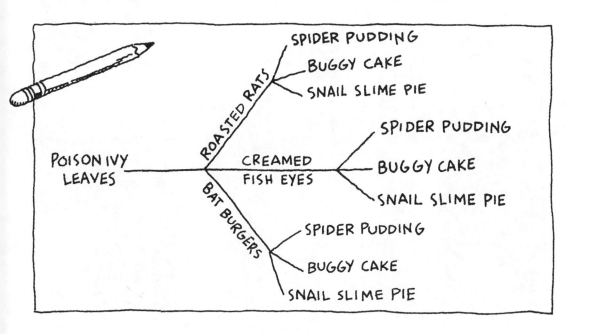

Liz for a game. How many lineups can you make? One way to find out is to shuffle the kids around, first forming as many lines as possible with one kid—Tom—at the head. After him, can come any of the other three, each of whom can be followed by either of the two others, who would be followed by the one who's left. If that's too much trouble, draw four kids' faces on filing cards and shuffle them around, keeping a record of each arrangement. Repeat this with each of the other three kids at the head of the line, and you'll be surprised at how many lineups are possible.

For an easier way to handle the problem, use arithmetic. You can get the answer by multiplying $4 \times 3 \times 2 \times 1$, which equals 24. But you don't even have to do that. If you use math shorthand, all you do is write 4!. That stands for the product of all the numbers from 4 down to 1. To say 4!, instead of writing it, don't bother catching your breath for that exclamation point. It stands for the word *factorial.* Just say, "Four factorial."

The number of possible lineups for five kids can be worked out in the same way:
$5 \times 4 \times 3 \times 2 \times 1$. That equals 120, or 5!. For six kids, the number would be 6!, and so on.

The number of possible arrangements of people or things grows very rapidly each time

another item is added, as this table shows.

Factorial Values

2! = 2	7! = 5,040
3! = 6	8! = 40,320
4! = 24	9! = 362,880
5! = 120	10! = 3,628,800
6! = 720	11! = 39,916,800

When you get up to 52!, the number of arrangements that can be made from a deck of 52 cards, the total is staggering. It's a figure with 68 digits. If all the people in the world counted a million arrangements a second, 24 hours a day, for 80 years, they couldn't count a billionth of a billionth of one-hundredth of the possibilities. So you see the advantage of counting without counting.

But what has all that to do with luck? For one thing, factorials are used in the formulas for figuring out the chances of getting certain combinations in lotteries or card games. Take the probability of picking six winning numbers out of 64 numbers in a lottery. This means finding how many six-number combinations there are in 64!. That comes to 25,827,166, giving each ticket holder one chance out of over 25 million to win. That's a very, very slim chance!

In bridge, each player is dealt 13 cards from a deck of 52. The total number of possible hands is 635,013, 559,600. But since four people play, the chance of anyone getting a particular hand is ¼ of that number, which comes to 1/158,753,389,900. That's such a slim chance you could play bridge around the clock all your life and still never get the same hand twice.

No wonder factorials make people say, "Wow!"

WIZARD OF ODDS

"Picking the odds" is related to figuring out probabilities, yet is not quite the same. People use the word *odds* in placing bets to show how much chance each side has of winning. Once you catch on to this, you can become a real Wizard of Odds.

LEARNING THE LINGO

Say you're about to toss coins with a friend. Both of you know that getting a head on one toss has a probability of ½. But in making your bet neither of you would say, "I'll bet a half." That wouldn't make sense. Since the chance of winning is equal to the chance of losing, both of you would bet the same amount. In other words, the odds would be one to one, which are written 1:1.

Now suppose you are throwing a die and bet that a 4 shows up. Although the probability for that is 1/6, the odds for winning the bet are 1:5, because there's one chance of getting a 4 to five chances of failing to get that number.

With two dice, both the odds and probability change. Each of a die's six sides can pair with each of the six sides of the other die, making 6 × 6, or 36, ways the dice can fall. But to get a 3 you need a 1 followed by 2 or 2 followed by 1. So the probability of a 3 is 2/36, or 1/18. And what are the odds? Since there are two chances of getting 3 against 34 of not getting it, the odds are 2:34 or 1:17.

When three dice are rolled, they can fall 216 different ways, and figuring out the odds for getting any sum becomes quite a job.

It really takes skill to become a wizard of odds.

It is said that the game of craps comes from ancient India. There, a group of people would play for a stake by taking turns throwing three dice until someone threw a 7 or 11 and became the winner. In the modern game, two dice are thrown and the rules are different.

THE THREE-CARD BET

The odds for winning are sometimes different from what people think they are. This helps hustlers pull off a fast deal with three cards: one black on both sides, one white on both sides and one black on one side but white on the other. After shaking the cards in a hat, the hustler gets someone to draw a card, set it on a table, and then bet on the color of the underside. He offers odds of 2:1 that the sides match. And more often than not, they do. He wins and collects the money the victim has bet.

People who watch the game usually think there's an equal

41

chance that the colors will match. They expect that the odds for guessing right are 1:1 and think the hustler's offer is a bargain. They cannot explain his success. Can you?

Here's how to figure it out:

Make a set of three cards, and play the game for peanuts with your friend, let's say, Joey. Offer odds of 2:1, betting two peanuts to one that the top of the card he draws matches the bottom side. Repeat this for six rounds and see how many peanuts you end up with. Then let Joey try his luck for six rounds. Keep a tally of the results.

You will find that when a card is chosen, the top and bottom sides are the same color about twice as often as they are different. To explain this, think of the possibilities. If the top side of a chosen card is black, it could be the top of the black-white card, or one side of the all black card, or the other side of that card. In two of these cases, both sides match; in one case, they do not. And you can bet on the match—2:1.

The kind of mistaken thinking that is often made in the three-card bet is like the mistake made in figuring the odds for any number when two dice are thrown. It's also like the mistake that's usually made in betting on how many heads or tails will show when two coins are tossed. (see page 19.)

SPEAKING OF MISTAKES

Scene: Airport Security Checkpoint. An inspector has just found a suspicious-looking black ball in a timid-looking man's suitcase.

Inspector: "This is a bomb!! Are you crazy?"

Man: "Just playing safe. They say the odds of a bomb on a plane are 1:1,000,000. So I have one with me to change the odds."

THE FIFTY-FIFTY CLUB

Peter stood blindfolded before the members of the Fifty-Fifty Club. Two covered bowls were set in front of him while the president explained, "Each bowl has 50 jellybeans in it—25 white ones and 25 black ones. That's a total of 100 beans. You pick a bowl, then I'll open it, and you pick one jellybean from it. If it's black, you can join. If it's white, you can't. Get it?"

"Sure," said Peter, grinning. "Fifty white, fifty black. So the odds are even." He did some quick thinking. Could he change the odds so that they would be in his favor? He really wanted to become a member of the club. Maybe there was a way to improve his chances of getting in.

"Do you ever make a switch?" he asked. "Why not put one black bean in one bowl and all the rest of the beans in the other bowl?"

"Why not?" the president replied.

No one objected and the jellybeans were rearranged.

Peter figured the change gave him a better chance to get into the club. Did it?

This is how Peter reasoned:
Before the switch, the chances of drawing a black jellybean from a bowl were 25 out of 50, giving a probability of ½, or odds of 1:1. Since this was the same for both bowls, it would not matter which one he chose.

With the new setup this was not true. One bowl now had 99 jellybeans in it—49 of them black. So the probability of picking a black one from it was 49/99. That's almost 50/100, or 1/2. But drawing a black bean from the other bowl was a sure thing, and in a case like that, the probability is always counted as 1.

To find the chance of getting a black bean from either of the two bowls, Peter averaged the two probabilities. He added 1 to ½ and divided by 2, which gave ¾. That meant the odds for picking a black bean in the new set up would be 3:1—three times better than the 1:1 odds in the old set up.

Well, what did Peter draw? A white jellybean.

"Tough luck," he said. "But I'm sure my math was right."

"I wish you'd explain it," said the president.

When Peter did, the club was very impressed, and the members voted to let him in anyway.

Then everybody ate the jelly-beans.

UPDATE ON THE RACE BETWEEN THE TURTLE AND THE HARE

You know the old story about the hare who fell asleep in the middle of a race with a turtle, and the slow-but-sure turtle won.

Not long ago, the animals arranged another race. This time the turtle was given a handicap to make the race fair. When it was found that hares are 20 times faster than turtles, the course was broken up into 10 laps, each 20 feet long. It was agreed that the hare was to start at the beginning of each lap, while the turtle would start at the 19-foot mark, and each lap was to be scored separately.

The odds were now 1:1, and a lot of animals were betting. They were surprised when the fox said, "Instead of betting on the outcome, I'll bet on the score at a given point in the race."

There were no takers until he offered odds of 5:1. Then the squirrel bet with him on condition that the fox write down his prediction before the race and put it in a sealed envelope. He did that.

And guess what happened.

The race was a tie. The only one to win was the fox. When the envelope with his score prediction was opened, the paper inside said:

Score at the beginning of the race: 0–0.

CLEVER PRINCESS II

Like movies, math teasers often have sequels and similar plots. In this one, King Babur the Bad still wants to marry Princess Cleo. Upon hearing she was planning a long trip, he passed a law forbidding people to leave the country. Cleo then begged him to let her go.

Finally, Babur said, "The law stands, but I shall let you choose between two silken bags. One holds a rare black bean; the other, a rare white bean. Choose the white one, and you can leave."

"What if I choose black?" asked Cleo.

"You stay and marry me. The drawing will take place tomorrow, supervised by my astrologer."

The astrologer leaked the story.

Soon many lords were betting 2:1 on a wedding. The ladies were betting there would not be one.

Convinced Babur would cheat, Cleo decided to outwit him.

And, of course, she did.

Cleo reasoned that Babur would put black beans in both bags. So when she drew a bean from one of the bags, she held it in her fist and started to cough. Being polite, she covered her mouth with her fist and swallowed the bean. When the astrologer emptied the other bag, all the ladies smiled. The bean that fell out was black.

Then what did Babur do? Stay tuned for Clever Princess III.

WIZ QUIZ

The answers are on the next page, but don't peek.

1. *Quick Pick:* **That's the name of a state lottery in which ticket holders choose six out of 36 numbers. What is the quickest way to find the odds for picking the six winning numbers?**

2. *Odds on the Odds:* **The numbers 1 through 7 are to be drawn from a hat. What are the odds the odd numbers will be drawn first?**

3. *Big Deal:* **Why is a bridge hand of 13 spades considered much more unusual than any other 13-card hand?**

4. *Nice Dice:* When 3 dice are rolled, are the odds of throwing a total of 6 twice as good as throwing a total of 3?

Answers:

1. *Quick Pick:* Look at the ticket. In every state with a lottery, odds are printed on all tickets sold.

2. *Odds on the Odds:* Since four out of seven numbers in the hat are odd, the probability that the first one drawn will be an odd is $4/7$. For the second one, it is $3/6$; for the third, $2/5$; for the fourth, $1/4$. Multiply those fractions and you get the probability for drawing the odd numbers. That comes to:
$$4/7 \times 3/6 \times 2/5 \times 1/4 = {}^{24}/_{840},$$
or $1/35$.
So the odds are only 1:34.

3. *Big Deal:* People think a hand of 13 cards in spades is very unusual because it's so striking. Actually, all hands are equally probable. Or you might say equally improbable, since the odds for getting any particular hand when four people play are 1:160,000,000,000.

4. *Nice Dice:* The odds are not twice as good—they are seven times as good. You get a 3 only with three 1s. But you can get a 6 in seven ways: 4, 1, 1; 1, 4, 1; 1, 1, 4; 3, 2, 1; 3, 1, 2; 1, 3, 2; 2, 2, 2.

LUCKY SNAP

You will need a friend and two decks of cards that are exactly alike for lucky snap. Better choose someone who won't mind losing—let's say, Marge.

Hand Marge a deck, tell her to shuffle it thoroughly, and place it face down on the table. You do the same with the second deck. Tell her to remove one card after another from her deck, and place it on the table, face up, while you do the same. If you both happen to draw the same card that's a snap.

At the beginning of the game, bet that you'll get a snap before you come to the end of the deck. You can offer odds of 2:1 and be reasonably sure of winning. In fact, you are likely to get a snap by the time you reach the thirteenth card. If you don't believe it, shuffle a deck of cards, then turn up the cards, one at a time, counting, "Ace, two, three, four . . . "going all the way to

king, and repeating this until the card you call matches the one you turn up. The chances are you won't have to repeat the count.

Try counting backward, and the result will be the same.

If you still don't believe it, make a pile of 13 cards running from ace through king, all of the same suit. Then make another pile like it, but of a different suit. Hand one pile to a friend, and both of you shuffle your cards. Then remove them one at a time, as in snap. Before you finish, the odds are 2:1 that you will draw two cards of the same value. The cards seem to be bewitched!

Why are the odds so high? You need advanced math to work out the answer. So if anyone asks you that question, dodge it. Just look superior and say, "It's hard to explain." Then quickly change the subject.

After all, you don't have to know *everything* to be a wizard of odds. You just have to know how to pick the right ones.

47

HOW FAIR IS FAIR?

An interesting problem arose in the days when European noblemen often gambled all night, playing for high stakes. Sometimes a game was interrupted after bets were made. Then arguments would start over the money in the jackpot. Was there a fair way to divide it?

The great French mathematician, Blaise Pascal, became interested in the problem and found a way of handling it. He said that each player's share of the jackpot should depend on how much of a chance he had to win, if the game had been played to the end.

What do you think? Ask a friend to play a game with a jackpot. Interrupt it. Then see if you can find a fair way to split the pot.

Here's a game to try. It's called dreidl. It's a game of luck that is centuries old. The dreidl is a four-sided top. Children spin it as they play for coins or candy during Hanukkah, a Jewish holiday that lasts eight days.

If neither you nor your friends have a dreidl, you can make one. Just cut a cardboard square, 3 inches wide. Print the letters G,M,H, and T on the sides. Draw diagonals across the square to locate the center and then push a sharpened pencil through it.

Two or three players can play. Each puts an agreed number of coins or candies in a jackpot and after drawing lots to see who starts first, the players take turns spinning the dreidl. From there

Hanukkah, the Jewish Festival of Lights, celebrates a miracle that supposedly took place over 2,000 years ago, when Hebrew priests and warriors recaptured a temple from invaders. There was hardly any oil to keep the temple lamps burning, but somehow the oil lasted for eight days.

Now, each side of the dreidl is marked G, M, H, or T, using English or Hebrew letters. In both cases, they are the first letters in the message: "A great miracle happened there."

on the rules vary, and many kids make up their own.

A good way to play is to score 1 point for G, 2 for M, 3 for H and no points for T, while keeping a record on a tally. The first one to get 10 points wins a round, and the winner of five rounds gets the jackpot.

Suppose that's the way you and your friend Sarah are playing Dreidl when the game is interrupted. Twelve counters are in the jackpot; Sarah has won 4 rounds; you have won 3. Now what should you do with the jackpot? If you divide it 4:3, Sarah would get 4/7 and you would get 3/7. It seems Sarah should get a better deal than that since she needs to win only one more round while you need two.

Yet, if the game continued, maybe Sarah would not win the next round. Maybe you would, and maybe you would win the round after that, too.

As things stand, Sarah's chances of winning are better than yours. You could decide on how to divide the jackpot if you knew how much better her chances are. But how do you figure them out?

Answer: At most, you would have to play two rounds to finish the game. That could lead to four possible outcomes. These are:

1. **Sarah wins the first round, but loses the second.**

2. **Sarah wins both rounds.**

3. **You win the first round but lose the second.**

4. **You win both rounds.**

As you see, you have only one chance out of four to win the jackpot, while Sarah has three out of four chances to win. The odds in Sarah's favor are 3:1. So she should get ¾ of the jackpot while you get ¼. That would be fair, wouldn't it?

BIRTHDAY BAFFLER

Is there anyone in your class at school whose birthday is the same as yours? If you are in a class with 23 or more kids, the odds are better than 1:1 that someone else was born on the same day of the same month as you. If there's a party, be prepared to share the honors.

Check on other large classes in your school. Probably you will find there are two kids with the same birthday in more than half of them.

The same holds true for groups of over 23 people of mixed ages.

So you can include teachers and the principal in your survey.

Mathematicians claim that the larger the group, the better the odds are for finding people with the same birthday. In a group of 50, it's almost a sure thing that at least two people were born on the same day of the year. The odds are better than 9:1.

How are those odds figured out? The math that's used is quite complicated. If you don't want to bother with it, just make the bet and collect. Probably no one will ask you to explain why you won.

If you are interested in how the odds are figured out, this will give you some idea of the way the problem is handled.

Let's take a group of 23. Ignoring leap years, the birthday of the first person in the group of 23 could be any one of 365 days. The probability for that is $\frac{365}{365}$. The probability that the second person in the group has a different birthday is $\frac{364}{365}$; for the third person, it is $\frac{363}{365}$; for the fourth birthday, it is $\frac{362}{365}$, and so on through the twenty-third person.

Now, the probability that all 23 have different birthdays is the product of the 23 fractions running from $\frac{365}{365}$ to $\frac{343}{365}$. For convenience, we'll use math shorthand and state the product as a decimal. This is what we get:

$$\frac{365}{365} \times \frac{364}{365} \times \frac{363}{365} \times \frac{362}{365} \cdots \frac{343}{365} = .493$$

The next step is simple, and it gives the answer. We just subtract that decimal from 1 which gives: 1 − .493 = .507

As you know, .507 is slightly better than ½. And that's the probability that at least two people out of the 23 have the same birthday. And that means the odds are a little better than 1:1.

The reason for the last step is interesting. According to the laws of chance, the probability that people in a group have different birthdays plus the probability that some of them have the same birthday equals 1. This can be turned around. So 1 minus our first probability—.493—equals the second probability—.507 —and that's the figure that solves our problem. Neat, isn't it?

POLLS AND PREDICTIONS

What are the chances something will happen? That's the big question in probability math—the mathematics of maybe. Lots of times people want to know not what *might* happen, but what actually *will* happen. Of course, it's helpful to know the chances, yet more facts may be needed to make a prediction. How can the facts be obtained? Are there any ways to tell what the future will bring? Let's find out.

MEET IMA PSYCHIC

Her real name isn't Ima, but like many psychics, she says she can see into the future and help people solve their problems. Although she may gaze into a crystal ball and read cards and even tea leaves, she relies on a special kind of ESP in making predictions. Or so she claims.

Her predictions are always vague. "A dark man will appear," she may say. Then she will go on with a series of events that could happen to anybody. The ones that don't come true are easily forgotten, but when something that was predicted does happen, Ima Psychic's reputation grows.

Psychics who make predictions for newspapers and magazines operate in the same way. A common prediction is that a TV star will soon get a divorce—and sure enough, one does. It's also certain that someone famous will die within a year. Many psychics made such a prediction the year President John Kennedy was shot. None of them said who would be killed, yet they all took credit for predicting the assassination.

Perhaps you can find a list made by a psychic. If you do, check it out. See for yourself how many prophecies come to pass.

CAN CARDS TELL YOUR FUTURE?

That "dark man" comes up again and again in fortunes told by cards. Many different card-reading systems are used. In most of them the fortune teller deals out 12 cards, placing them face down in 4 rows, 3 in a row. The cards supposedly stand for the 12 months of the year, and the rows for the four weeks in a month.

While laying out the cards, the fortune-teller finds out the questions to be answered. The person seeking the answers then picks a card from the deck and lays it face up on a card already on the table. Then the fortune-teller studies the two cards. The routine is repeated for each question.

What do the cards mean? Where a card is placed is supposed to tell the date of a future event. Its value tells who will be on the scene, and the suit tells what that person will be like.

Here are some meanings often given to the cards:

For the face cards

ace—high achiever
king—man, perhaps a big shot
queen—woman
jack—young man

For suits

clubs—strength
hearts—friendship, love
spades—industriousness
diamonds—talent for making money

CLEVER PRINCESS III

King Babur's astrologer and Princess Cleo were enemies. She knew he faked forecasts to please Babur. Since the astrologer knew she knew, he planned to kill her. Cleo was aware of this.

What could Cleo do? Perhaps she could destroy his power. She formed a plan when she heard that the astrologer was going to make a special forecast of Babur's future and read the king's horoscope at his birthday party.

Cleo knew how a horoscope is made. The astrologer finds out

As card after card is turned up, the fortune-teller adds a little here and there and weaves together an interesting story.

Try telling a friend's fortune. See what you come up with. Then try a second reading. Maybe it will contradict the first. In any case, it won't be the same. In a 52-card deck, the number of 12-card combinations is about 20,000,000,000,000,000. That's 20 quadrillion!

the position of several heavenly bodies on a person's birth date, decides how they affect his or her life, and then forecasts that person's future. After talking this over with some friends, Cleo set her trap.

And what do you think she did?

At the birthday party, trumpets blared. Then the astrologer read the king's horoscope for the coming year. Babur, he said, was born under the sign of Leo the Lion. That meant he would have health, wealth, and happiness, and he would triumph in love and war.

The court clapped politely. Smiling sweetly, Princess Cleo stood up and said, "Cheers for Babur and cheers for my three friends whose future should be like the king's, for today is their birthday, too."

Three lords stood and bowed. An uproar followed. The astrologer managed to escape. Babur was in a rage. But Cleo continued to smile and tossed kisses to her three friends: Lord Weaknee who was so sick he could hardly stand, Lord Richard who had just gone bankrupt, and Lord Lovelace whose wife had left him that very day—Lions, one and all.

ASTROLOGY FUNOLOGY

If you are curious about your astrological sign, look for a horoscope column in your local newspaper. Nearly every daily newspaper in the United States has one. So do many monthly magazines.

If you compare two or more of these columns, you will find that their predictions often contradict each other. Not only that, their predictions are like the forecasts of psychics and fortune-tellers. They are worded so that you can interpret them any way you want.

Probably other kids in your school have the same birthday that you have (see *Birthday Baffler*, page 50). Get together, if you can, and see how different you are. Then read a horoscope for your sign. If success is predicted for you, just smile. But don't count on it (and that goes for a prediction of bad luck, too!).

Astrologers place great importance on 12 constellations appearing in a part of the sky called the *zodiac*. These constellations are called: Taurus the Bull, Gemini the Twins, Cancer the Crab, Leo the Lion, Virgo the Virgin, Libra the Scales, Scorpio the Scorpion, Sagittarius the Archer, Capricorn the Goat, Aquarius the Water Carrier, Pisces the Fish, and Aries the Ram. During the year, the sun rises and sets in the neighborhood of the constellations, one after another. It seems to spend about a month in each one.

Astrologers call each constellation in the zodiac a *sign* and they claim that each sign affects fate. Anyone born when the sun rose in Taurus should be like a bull. Anyone born in Libra should be just. So people with the same birthday should be very much alike.

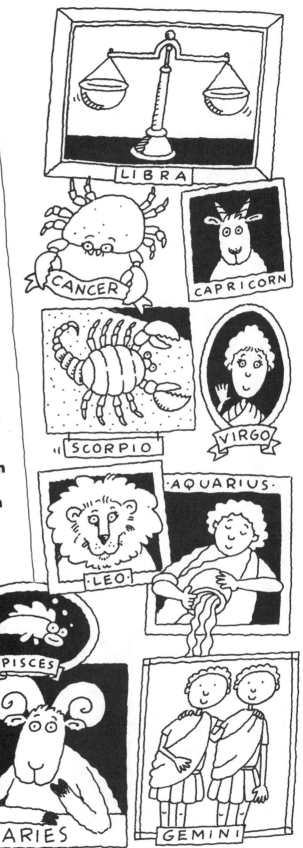

MOON WATCH

Is any kind of forecasting reliable?

Look in your newspaper for a box telling the expected dates of the moon's four phases—new moon, first quarter, full moon, and second quarter. Or look for those predictions in an almanac. Check them whenever you can, and you'll find they are accurate.

As it happens, astrologers were

responsible for them. Long ago, they watched the skies night after night. Thinking that the sun, moon, and planets were gods, astrologers kept records of their movements and used the records to foretell when and where these heavenly bodies would appear. The predictions were so accurate that people thought their own futures could be predicted, too. That seemed reasonable back in the days when no one knew much about any of the heavenly bodies, but it makes no sense today.

WEATHER PREDICTIONS

Today: fair weather; *Tomorrow:* 60 percent probability of rain. Have you heard forecasts like that on TV? When such a forecast is made, the announcer is letting you know that the chances for rain are six out of 10, although the prediction for fair weather is a sure thing.

Accurate predictions can be made for many kinds of weather, but not for all. The air keeps changing in more ways than the Weather Bureau can keep track of. Besides, some of the changes that take place are not well understood. Even so, daily forecasts for local areas are right more than eight times out of ten.

See for yourself. Compare the

daily forecasts with the weather for a week, and you will find that the predictions are usually accurate.

APPLE PIE—YUM-YUM

There is an old story about a baker who wanted to be sure that his pies were the best in town. So he ate one to find out if it was any good. *Yum-yum*, it was good. But he was not sure that the others were good. So he ate another pie, and another pie. Yes, they were good, but still he was not sure of the rest. So he kept on eating pie after pie, until there were none left to sell.

Alas, the poor baker. How could he have learned that his pies were the best in town without eating them all?

Answer: The baker could have taken a sample. That is, he could have eaten some of the pies, perhaps one out of every 20. If they were all made in the same way, and the pies he ate were good, the probability is high that the other pies would be good, too.

Modern bakers test their products that way. So do many manufacturers. In making light bulbs, there would be none to sell if each one was tested. until it burned out. Instead a certain number of bulbs is picked at random from a batch and tested. Then the test results are used in making a probability calculation. This gives the manufacturer a pretty good idea of how long the other bulbs in the batch will last.

POP TEST

A fun way to do some sample testing is to check a cupful of raw popcorn and find out how much of it can be expected to pop. But before starting, be sure an adult is around to help you.

For the sample, take 1 teaspoon of kernels from the cup, and count them. Say it holds 40 kernels. A cup holds 48 teaspoons, so you will be testing $\frac{1}{48}$ of a batch. For the test, pour 1 teaspoon of vegetable oil into a small frying pan, then add the sample and heat it. Keep shaking the pan until most of the kernels have popped. Then turn off the heat, remove the kernels that didn't pop with a spoon, and count them. Say four did not pop. That's $\frac{4}{40}$, or $\frac{1}{10}$ of the sample. So you can say the probability for duds in the batch is $\frac{1}{10}$.

Meanwhile you can eat the other 36 kernels.

How about the rest of the kernels? Test another teaspoonful. Then another. Can you rely on your test for "popability probability"?

PICKING AT RANDOM

Suppose you were testing light bulbs and had to pick one out of six at random. That would mean picking some bulbs that were the first of every six coming off the assembly line, some that were the second, and so on. How would you manage that?

One mathematician said he would throw a die and pick a bulb every time a six came up. And that method would be as good as any, if the bulbs were to be picked by hand. Actually, bulbs to be tested are picked by a device that stops them at different intervals.

Sometimes telephone numbers are picked at random to find people who might buy something or answer questions for an advertiser. Then a long list of the numbers is prepared. Looking at the list, and the last four digits in each number, you would expect each of the digits from 1 through 9 to show up equally often. But they don't. The digit 1 occurs most often; 2 is also common; 8 and 9 are much less common.

Phone-number digits are not scattered helter-skelter. They tend to form a pattern. In all, 1, 2, 3, and 4 are more common than the other digits in phone numbers. This is also true of the digits in the numbers on nearly all long lists.

See for yourself. Ask four people to take the first 20 numbers on a page in the phone book and list the last 4 digits in them. You will then have a list of 20 × 4 × 4, or 320 digits. Strike out every 1, 2, 3, and 4. Count the number you struck out. Does it come to more than half of the 320 digits listed?

Check lists of numbers from an almanac or an atlas and see how the digits in them run. Want to bet you will find more digits under 5 than over 5? Mathematicians can explain this—but not in simple terms.

QUICK COUNTING

Samples are useful, not only in tests, but when you are making counts. Once you know that 40 kernels of popcorn are in a teaspoon, you can tell the number in a cup without counting them all. Since a cup holds 48 teaspoons, the total number of kernels in it probably is 40 × 48, or 1,920.

This method is known as quick counting. It is quite accurate if you use a typical sample. If the kernels in your sample are small ones from the top of the package, the total will be too high. If they are big ones from the bottom, it will be too low. But you can avoid such mistakes. Just mix the batch. Then take several samples from it and use the average number in them when you figure the total for the batch.

Try a quick count of the number of letters in 10 lines on this page, and you will see how the method works.

Every time you have a blood test, a sample is taken and used in a quick count of your red and white blood cells. Each quart of blood normally has 5 trillion red cells and nearly 9 billion white cells in it. You have at least three quarts of blood in your body. Even though the sample used for a test is about a millionth part of a quart, a doctor can tell from it whether you have normal, healthy blood.

HOW DO PUBLIC OPINION POLLS WORK?

A public opinion poll is really a kind of quick counting. A certain number of people are asked to give their opinions on different topics. Then the opinions collected in the poll are treated as a sample that supposedly shows what a large group of people think.

Suppose the people planning a school lunch program want to know if spinach is popular. It would take too much time to ask all the boys and girls in the school. So they decide to ask only a few and take a poll.

Who will be asked, "Do you like spinach?" If only eighth graders are asked, they would all be about the same age. Younger children would be left out, and they are the ones who often don't like vegetables. A better plan would be to select boys and girls from every class. This could be done by writing the names of everyone in the school on slips of paper, putting all the slips in a barrel, and then taking out 50 names at random.

Will everyone answer the question honestly? Answers sometimes depend on who is asking the questions. A child is likely to give one answer to a young person and another answer to someone who is older. A boy might not give the same answer to a man as to a woman.

The way a question is asked is important, too. Suppose the pollster says, "You like spinach, don't you?" A child may say, "Yes" without thinking. But "Do you like spinach?" might bring a more honest answer.

And probably some of those questioned don't care one way or another about spinach. So there should be another possible answer: "I don't care."

It's not easy to take a poll that gives reliable results. But perhaps you and your friends might like to try one. If you do, think of some issue that's important to your schoolmates—something more interesting than spinach. How about this: Should boys and girls play together on baseball teams?

If you ask that kind of question—or any other kind, for that matter—both boys and girls should be pollsters. Will the boys get different answers than the girls? It will be fun to find out.

PREDICTING ELECTION RESULTS

Some years ago, a magazine, the *Literary Digest,* had a poll to find out if the public favored Franklin Roosevelt, who was running for president for the first time, or Alfred Landon, his opponent. Roosevelt was a Democrat; Landon, a Republican. The *Digest* sent out ten million letters with poll questions, and two million people replied. The majority of them wrote they favored Landon. Yet Roosevelt won by a landslide. Why? The majority of people who took part in the poll were Republicans.

That kind of mistake is avoided

today. To get a typical mixture of people, pollsters use phone books and other lists from various parts of the country. Then they pick every hundredth name or number, or perhaps fewer than that, for their sample.

But a poll is not an election. In a poll, sample opinions are collected. In an election, ballots are given to everyone who turns out to vote. Yet experts can usually predict the winners long before all the ballots are counted.

How do they do it? They watch the returns hour by hour and spot trends. If they see one candidate keeps running far ahead of another, they expect him or her to continue leading. They then predict the winner. And usually they are right.

INDEX